BLOOD THIRST

BLOOD THIRST

THE TRUE STORY OF WAYNE BODEN: VAMPIRE, RAPIST, SERIAL KILLER

ALAN R. WARREN

BLOOD THIRST: The True Story of Wayne Boden - Vampire, Rapist, Serial Killer
Written by Alan R. Warren

Published in Canada

Copyright @ 2020 by Alan R. Warren

All rights reserved. No part of this book may be reproduced, scanned, or distributed in any printed or electronic form without permission of the author. The unauthorized reproduction of a copyrighted work is illegal. Criminal copyright infringement, including infringement without monetary gain, is investigated by the FBI and is punishable by fines and federal imprisonment. Please do not participate in or encourage privacy of copyrighted materials in violation of the author's rights. Purchase only authorized editions.

This is a work of nonfiction. No names have been changed, no characters invented, no events fabricated.

Cover design, formatting and layout by Evening Sky Publishing Services

BOOK DESCRIPTION

Known as the "Vampire Rapist" or "Strangler Bill" for his distinctive modus operandi (MO), Wayne Boden would rape, strangle and bite the breasts of his victims.

His murdering rampage would continue in two cities over three years; he was only caught by superior evidence gathering and the help of an orthodontist. This book asks the question, "How do we really know our boyfriend or lover when we don't want to ask the questions, not only because we don't want to know the answers for what it will tell us about them, but because of what it tells us about ourselves?"

True Crime Author Alan R. Warren takes you through the details of the case including the dental impressions used in court to convict Boden, a first in Canadian history, as well as Boden's escape from a maximum-security prison.

CONTENTS

Foreword	ix
Introduction	xi
1. Humble Beginnings of Boden	1
2. Vive Le Quebec	7
3. Death of Norma Vaillaincourt	15
4. Ball Of Confusion	21
5. Murder of Shirley Audette	27
6. Murder of Marielle Archambault	33
7. Murder of Jean Way	39
8. Go West Young Man	43
9. The Murder of Elizabeth Porteous	53
10. Trial of Wayne Boden	61
Afterword	73
Epilogue	79
Acknowledgments	85
About the Author	87
Also by Alan R. Warren	89
References	91

FOREWORD

BY JUDITH A. YATES | AWARD-WINNING TRUE CRIME AUTHOR & CRIMINOLOGIST

German psychiatrist Richard von Kraft-Ebing introduced both the terms "sadistic" and "masochism" in 1890. According to Sigmund Freud, inflicting and receiving pain for sexual gratification "is the most common and important of all perversions." Both Kraft-Ebing and Freud would have had an excellent prototype in serial killer Wayne Boden.

Wayne Clifford Boden (c. 1948 –2006), a Canadian serial killer known to be active during 1969-1971, was dubbed "The Vampire Rapist" for his penchant of biting the victim's breasts and enjoying the experience of tasting the blood. It was one of these bites that led to the investigation and then the arrest of Boden that landed him in prison; Boden was ensconced in Kingston Penitentiary, residing there briefly until his slick con game gave him access to an American Express credit card, forcing a billion dollar company to examine just how a man convicted for life in prison obtained perfect credit.

This is a story of all things that make true crime interesting and educating. Boden's was the first North American conviction based on forensic odontology, before Ted Bundy's trial made the investigative practice common knowledge. Thus, his story is one of breakthrough forensic work. Using the name "Bill" he managed to charm and woo innocent women, some of them paying for their trust with an early grave. Boden's personality gives insight into how a sadistic, evil mind can so easily be masked by good looks and charm. Friends of the last victim gave the best lead in identifying "Bill," ultimately leading to the arrest, an example of the policeman's best crime fighting tool: witnesses.

Kraft-Ebing and Freud were adept at introducing the sadomasochist; Alan R. Warren is adept at telling this story of Wayne Clifford Boden. Alan offers distinct insight into true crime stories because of his work as show host and producer of the popular *House of Mystery* talk show (heard on KKNW 1150 A.M.) Alan knows what questions to ask, revealing the inside stories. He is as good at listening as he is at telling; equally important tools when writing true crime.

INTRODUCTION

Do we really know the people around us such as our neighbors, friends, coworkers or even our partners and lovers? Why is it that so many people are blinded to what's right in front of them? Is it that we really don't see it, or is it that we just don't want to see it, like a form of denial? When we consider the face of someone that we know, are we focusing on their eyes, lips or nose or are we looking beyond that to what's inside of them and their minds? Are they kind, true and really loving, or is there a dark side that we really are ignoring or just trying to avoid? It has been said that what we dislike most in others is what we really dislike about ourselves.

Even when we hear things about the people we know, we just don't ask more questions or try to go deep. Perhaps we just don't want to know any more information about that person, or is it that we just don't want to ask the questions because we might find out something about ourselves that we don't want to face? Is it that we really don't want to know, or do we think that we are not going to be able to deal with what we find out? Perhaps when we do learn this information, it will change the way that we live our lives forever. When we are living among psychopaths in our daily lives, is there any way that we can tell them apart from non-psychopaths? Do we have enough skills to be a judge of character that we would know immediately if someone that we were around was a psychopath?

I must ask myself why is it that whenever I do interviews for my radio show about serial killers or write a book about one, the family, friends and coworkers always are so surprised, and say "he could never do such a thing." Or they look back upon the time that they had spent knowing the person and start to remember things that were weird about that person but at the time never questioned their behavior.

Quite often when we hear about a vampire killer, the person that comes to mind is Richard Chase known as "The Vampire Serial Killer of Sacramento." He killed six people in the span of one month, cannibalizing their remains and drinking their blood. Chase showed signs of psychological problems early on in his life, then became an alcoholic and chronic drug user.

He started his vampire attacks beginning in December of 1977 and, by January 1978, his reign was over. He was convicted of six counts of murder in the first degree and was sentenced to die in the gas chamber. He ended up killing himself in prison in December of 1980 with prescribed anti-depressants.

But there was another vampire killer, not only before Richard Chase, but in the quiet, unexpected country of Canada, by the name of Wayne Boden. A sexual sadist who was obsessed with the desire to bite female breasts,

Boden became known as "The Vampire Rapist" from his chilling method of murder.

Prowling the streets of Montreal, he staged a two-year reign of terror with attacks that outraged the community for their brutal animal-like ferocity. Wayne Boden would then continue his reign of terror in the city of Calgary.

Why was this case not as well-known as Richard Chase? I tend to connect to us not wanting to know certain things about what other humans do. We just don't want to know, and just won't ask the questions. This book will lay out the brutal behavior from the beginning of Wayne Boden and how he almost got away.

Wayne Boden had dark beautiful eyes that served as his disguise, on a dangerous face. By the end of it all, he was left with no life, except for the blood on his hands. Did he know the reasons why he was a beautiful killer? Maybe this was his version of together until death do we part or hold on to them until there's nothing left. After all, he only would make such attacks on the women that had the potential to become his wife. How far were these women willing to go to finally find love and a husband? How much longer could he carry these sins on his back after he committed such crimes?

When we are young, we tend to trade our love for the possibility of fame, power or riches. It all becomes a game, not realizing that there are some things that we just can't buy. We run far away from the home that we grew up in, just to travel the world looking for a new home, wanting it so badly that we will trust almost anyone that we think could offer this dream to us. Even when we are scared and run into something bad for us, we keep going back for more. We hit every famous destination, far-off places, and talk to any strangers that will listen in the night.

How can we trust what we feel in this world with so many souls that come from a tortured beginning? How do we spot this in somebody that we know and love, never mind somebody that we have just met? Why is it that we can open to someone that's attractive to ourselves, and we don't even know their name?

What triggered this behavior in Wayne Boden? Was it the continuous neglect in early home life that such behavior was taught? Alienated character, we don't want to know what's in front of us, or ask the questions that would tell us. There is a definite connection between all of us, so if we are not looking deeper, closer at the others around us, are we ever going to find out or know what's about to come? Profound sexual and physical abuse is not required to commit these kinds of acts. It's so much easier to just think of him as a monster.

Do I know you from somewhere before? Why do you leave me wanting more? You've got this thing that I can't explain, soon becomes we've got this thing we can't explain. As soon as we meet we have a desire to make a connection. I think that we are walking on a thin line, but we just close our eyes and jump in.

One would never expect that such a smooth talker, well turned out and good looking person could commit such violent crimes.

1

HUMBLE BEGINNINGS OF BODEN

"We come to Beginnings only at the End" –
William Throsby Bridges

Wayne Clifford Boden was born on January 1, 1948. He grew up in the quiet tree-lined streets of Dundas, Ontario. Located only 13 miles west of Hamilton, Ontario in the picturesque Dundas Valley, it was a town with historic 19th century buildings and a population of about 12,000 people in the 1960's. It was known as the home of the famous comedian of SCTV Dave Thomas and Major League Baseball pitcher Pete Ward.

Wayne's father, Albert, died in 1966 when Wayne was 18 years old. He wasn't close with his father, who was very strict and not known as very affectionate. He had worked in a factory for 30 years. Wayne's mother, Laverna, would have been 34 when she gave birth to him. She was the consummate housewife and believed her goal in life was to keep a well-run home, clean, and always have the dinner on the table at the same time every night.

Laverna was not close to her son at all; she was more of a school headmistress than mother to Wayne, only communicating with nothing but duties for him to perform. Laverna was never known to give a kind word to anybody and constantly complained about how people never knew how to do their jobs correctly. An example would be how she would always tell the milkman how he had got their order wrong, delivered too-warm milk, and was always late for his delivery.

Wayne was not close to his mother and didn't really like her. She was not an educated woman and couldn't read or write at all. He found himself always having to help her with these things in her duties as a housewife, such as writing up the order for the milkman. Sometimes he would find himself frustrated with her and thought that she was stupid, and he was embarrassed by this.

He found himself telling the teachers at school that his mother was not alive because he didn't want to tell them about her. Why couldn't his mother be like his teachers? Not only were they women, but they were smart and could read and write.

Wayne's parents had never shown any signs of affection in front of him. He was never allowed into their bedroom; it was one of many rooms that was simply out of bounds for him to enter. The main living room and kitchen were also off limits to him. It was a very isolating experience for Wayne.

It was an accident the first time that he had caught a glimpse into his parents' room. He was outside of their doorway when his mother came out with a large load of sheets in her arms, and she was unable to close the door right away. He noticed that there were two beds in the room. This was not an uncommon practice in the 1950s and '60s. Quite often the master room would be furnished with two twin beds, not the standard double or queen-size beds of today. Even on the popular television shows or movies of the time, the main characters always had twin beds portrayed in their bedrooms.

This one quick glimpse led Wayne to fantasize on how it must be to be married. He developed the idea that you only would sleep with your wife when you were trying to have children and that the wife's duty was simply to run the household, almost more of a job and not a loving relationship. This was probably where he started to put the placing of a woman as second to the man in the house.

Wayne did not have any brothers or sisters either. He would come home right after school, as his mother would be watching to see what time he would arrive. If he was late even by five minutes, she would scold him for taking his time when he had work to do.

After his list of chores were completed, he would show up for his dinner, which was exactly at five thirty, and she would first check to see that his hands had been washed before he could even sit at the table. Dinner would then be served, and the three of them would sit and eat in silence, with the only noise being the sound of their grandfather clock ticking in the dining room, that Wayne had never been allowed in. He knew the clock by sound far better than he ever would have by sight.

After he would finish dinner and be excused from the table, he would go straight into his room and close his door. He would not see his parents again until morning.

His mother would walk down the hall and stop at his door at 8 p.m. every night and listen. He would just lie there silent, even holding his breath, careful not to make any noise, or she would yell at him that it was time to be asleep. After she walked away and went into her own bedroom, he would resume his activities.

Wayne always spent his nights alone in his room, never inviting anyone over. He didn't want to have to deal with bringing somebody into his home and having them face his mother. Not only that, he never had any close friends in his school days, so there was nobody to invite.

He would just lie on his bed listening to CKOC AM 1150 out of Hamilton on his transistor radio alone. He liked hearing the latest in music, and he would close his eyes and dream that it was him singing the song. He had this fantasy that he was going to become a popular pop artist and all the pretty girls would stand in long lines waiting to hear him sing. There is no record of him ever trying to learn to sing, or him being part of the music or theatre department at school. Instead, he ended up joining the football team at school.

Boden went to Glendale secondary school until the mid-1960s. He was thought of as quiet, muscular, and played on the school senior football team. He was well liked by his teachers, as he was respectful and quiet. Wayne seemed to admire his teachers and always went out of his way to help them as much as he could. He would clean their chalk boards, carry books, and quite often stay behind to help in any way that he could. This affection towards teachers would take a twist in the very near future, not anything that people would expect.

Wayne's nice, helpful behavior towards his teachers

was not something a lot of other students in the school appreciated. Though he was liked by most other students, the most misbehaved students thought of Wayne as a 'suck up' or 'teacher's pet' and would always call him names. Wayne, being a football player with the tough reputation that came with that, almost forced him to stand up for himself against such ridicule. He would find himself getting into several fights at school, one of them quite bloody with fellow student George Tirone in which Boden was the winner.

Wayne tried his luck at being a model; he was handsome, well-built and clean cut. Most of the girls in school would comment how handsome he was. But Wayne was extremely shy, would never look people in the eyes. He would also not talk much; many times at parties he would sit by himself in the corner of the room and could go unnoticed for hours. Wayne never had any girlfriends during his high school days. It is more likely that he wasn't secure enough to ask any girl to go out with him.

This kind of attitude was not very conducive with being a model. He was also extremely shy about taking off his clothes. Though he was nicely built, he felt the need to keep himself covered completely and wouldn't even shower with the other boys after playing football. Consider that being a model would mean he would have to be more aggressive and face the camera, and certainly not be afraid of taking off his shirt, or more. Additionally, there were just no modeling jobs in this small town.

He then tried different sales positions around town, but again, being such a small town, there just wasn't much opportunity.

Wayne found it very hard to make any sales when his

customer base was so small. He felt he would have to move to a larger city, but didn't know where. At first, he tried Hamilton, which was a short distance from home, and certainly a much bigger center to work in. But Wayne grew tired of Hamilton rather quickly. Hamilton, though it was larger, didn't have the culture base that he was looking for. Hamilton was known as a steel town. It was Canada's version of Pittsburgh, where the base of the economy was steel manufacturing. With that came a lot of steel workers and their families that were not looking for nightlife, parties and male models.

Wayne had not adjusted very well. He was extremely awkward around others and couldn't hold a conversation for any length of time. His father died when he was young, and his mother was quite a bit older. Not having any brothers or sisters, he spent most of his time alone, with no social interaction.

It was sometime in 1967 when Wayne moved to Montreal to 1849 Dorch #24 and worked as a travelling salesman. He maintained his well-built frame from his high school football days, with the current trend of bushy sideburns. Considered to be mild-mannered and very polite, he was the kind of man that you could take home to your parents. Moving to the big city also gave him lots of young people to meet and clubs in which to socialize.

2

VIVE LE QUEBEC

"I Want to go Where the People Dance, I Want Some Action, I Want to live, I Love the Nightlife, I Got to Boogie" - Alicia Bridges

Montreal, Quebec is a city well known around the world for its art, culture and nightlife. It was the second largest metropolis in Canada with over three million residents. In fact, Montreal had a long history as the place to go for cabarets.

During the prohibition act of the 1920s, when most American cabarets were going bankrupt, the Quebec government saw an opportunity. They created "La Commission des Liqueurs du Quebec", which allowed legal, but controlled access to, alcohol for everyone of legal age, which in Quebec was 20 years of age. In 1972, it was lowered to 18 years old and has maintained that age since. The legal age to vote has followed the legal age to drink, and it was lowered to 18 as well.

PROHIBITION IN CANADA

Prohibition was mostly spurred by the efforts of people in the temperance movement, which wanted to have all drinking establishments closed. They viewed alcohol as the source of societal ills and misery. The temperance movement established itself through much of the United States and Canada. One of the core values of the temperance movement was the complete abolition of alcohol and it attempted to spread its message in every manner possible.

In 1878, Canada passed the Canada Temperance Act, which provided an option for each province to decide if they would allow a prohibition scheme in their province. The federal government decided to have a referendum on the subject in which all provinces except for Quebec approved of the idea of prohibition. In Quebec, it was quite the opposite, where 81.2 % voted against it.

By the first world war in 1918, every province had made the decision to enforce prohibition in their respective provinces due to the added pressure to preserve grain for the demands of World War 1. The Canadian War Measures Act of 1918 enforced the Canadian prohibition to which there were only two exceptions:

1. Ontario still allowed the production of alcohol strictly for export sales only. Exporting the alcohol to the United States was referred to as "Rum-running." Rum-running was simply

using a boat to carry the alcohol from Windsor, Ontario to Detroit, Michigan,
2. Quebec's Provincial Government passed their own law allowing the legal sales of alcohol to anyone that was of legal age in the province.

This led to a large amount of cabarets to open around the southern part of St. Laurent Boulevard, which was fueled by the New York scene. Various types of performers and artists headed to Montreal where they could find work.

By the 1930s, the infamous Mary Louise Cecilia "Texas" Guinan moved to Montreal, the notorious actress, singer and queen of the New York underground nightlife. By Guinan coming to Montreal and performing her very popular numbers, there started a craze for the Montreal nightlife. Massive crowds from all over North America headed to Montreal to partake in its risqué nightlife.

By 1940, there were well over 30 cabarets operating in the downtown core of the city. With the American prohibition now repealed, you might think that Montreal would have been hit hard, but it was quite the opposite.

The cabaret and red light district kept growing and did not peak until well after World War 2. It wasn't until sometime in the mid 1950s that televisions started entering people's homes, and the need to go out for entertainment no longer existed. There was also a conservative swing then as the mayor of Montreal, Jean Drapeau, created the "Comite de Moralite Publique de Montreal," which was the public morality committee. This resulted in many arrests and closure of many cabarets and gaming houses in Montreal.

By the 1960s, the cabarets that were left in business

were forced to clean up their image. They were under great competition with each other and had to come up with new ideas to attract clientele. Most cabarets started to bring in French and American stars to perform, such as Frank Sinatra, Jerry Lewis, Dean Martin and Edith Piaf. The atmosphere was changing slightly to where the clubs would now fill up with everyone eager to watch these new kinds of acts and socialize until the early hours of the morning, and possibly lead to new romances.

In 1967, the World's Fair Expo '67 came to Montreal, bringing millions of people from around the world to the city. The World's Fair is a large international exhibition designed to showcase achievements of nations. These exhibitions vary in character and are held in varying cities throughout the world. The best known and first world expo was held in Crystal Palace in Hyde Park, London, United Kingdom in 1851.

The Montreal Expo started on April 27 and lasted until October 29. Actually, it was at the Montreal World's Fair named "Man and His World" that they officially changed the name of the World's Fair to Expo '67. The name was also used for the professional baseball team in Montreal, the Montreal Expos.

There was an estimated crowd of between 300,000 and 335,000 people that came for opening day. The fair attracted a lot of attention with artists like the Supremes, Petula Clark, Grateful Dead, Tiny Tim, Jefferson Airplane, and even Ed Sullivan broadcast his show from there twice. The fair was attended by many famous people of the time, the most notable of them including Queen Elizabeth II, Lyndon B. Johnson, Princess Grace of Monaco, Robert F. Kennedy, Jacqueline Kennedy, Charles

De Gaulle, Bing Crosby, Harry Belafonte, and Marlene Dietrich.

Despite the success, there were also problems that started to plague Montreal. When President Lyndon B. Johnson came to the opening ceremony, Vietnam war protesters picketed. There were threats that the Cuba pavilion would be destroyed by anti-Castro forces.

In June, the Arab-Israel conflict in the Middle East flared up again in the Six Day War, which resulted in Kuwait pulling out of the fair in protest to the way that the western nations dealt with the war.

At the height of the fair in July, Charles De Gaulle caused an international incident when he addressed thousands at the Montreal City Hall by yelling out the now famous words "Vive Montreal," "Vive le Quebec," and "Vive Le Quebec Libre." (Long Live Free Quebec) This also led the official separatists party to send bomb threats to the fair regularly from this point on.

But the most serious problem to the fair was in September when the public transit staged a 30-day strike. The original estimate for visitors was at 60 million, but the strike cut into the attendance deeply.

Not only was the city very festive with the World's Fair, but it was also the 100th birthday of the Dominion of Canada, celebrating the process of becoming a separate nation from England.

It was around this time that Wayne Boden decided to move to Montreal where everything was happening and the options of work and becoming a model could happen. He moved into an apartment at 1849 Dorchester #24. The apartment was small, but cozy, and, best of all, well hidden from the view of the road by a bushy tree. It was also centrally located in the city in an area called the Dorchester Square. The square was a high foot traffic district lined with dark sidewalk cafes and close to much of the festivities in town.

It would not be long before Wayne would head out to the street and stand amongst what seemed to be thousands of people, all walking around him, mainly speaking in French. He would stand still in the middle of the sidewalk, close his eyes, and let the crowds walk around him as if he wasn't even there. This seemed to give him a thrill; with his eyes closed, he would be forced to sense people's presence by their voices and smells, and he tried very hard to concentrate on the sounds around him. This could easily have been his early training on reading people and learning to pay close attention to details.

Though he was very polite, friendly and approachable, he very seldom engaged with others. That kind of human behavior certainly doesn't fit with being a model or salesman, and that might just be why he was not successful at either, even though in his mind it was because he had lived in such a small town where there was no opportunity. He knew that he had no problem catching the attention of both men and women, but he couldn't figure out why. His shyness helped in that. It was almost like a person that doesn't like cats – they are always the first to attract them.

He started out as a travelling salesman, which was great, as you would visit people one on one when performing your sales presentation. He was best at this sort of procedure, as he had no problem engaging a person. It was crowds or larger groups of people that he didn't feel comfortable speaking in front of.

He would spend most of his time off in his apartment. He had a 1967 Zenith Record Stereo Player console cabinet and played records like 'Light my Fire" by The Doors repeatedly, with his eyes closed and imagining himself in other places, and being other people. He would even think that he was Jim Morrison singing to a crowd of women that worshiped him. It wouldn't be long before he would take this fantasy out into the public and introduce it to others.

DEATH OF NORMA VAILLAINCOURT

"If you wear a mask for too long, there will come a time when you cannot remove it without removing your face." – Matshona Dhliwayo

The summer of 1967 was unusually hot in Montreal, recording some of the hottest temperatures on record. Another newcomer to the city was Norma Vaillaincourt, who came originally from a rural community in Quebec, Canada called Sainte-Anne-de-Beaupre. This was a very small town about 30 miles northeast of Quebec City. It had a population of only about 500 people in 1970.

Norma was a 21-year-old school teacher but needed to complete more classes to further her career. Montreal was the closest city that offered such courses, so she had packed up her belongings and moved. She was not married yet and did not have a boyfriend. She never had any luck in her hometown with dating. It seemed all the men just wanted to stay and be farmers and raise families. Norma wanted so much more than that. She wanted to have a family, this was true, but she also wanted to pursue teaching and college.

Norma rented an apartment by herself in the east end of town, on Davidson Street. This was a working-class part of Montreal and was one of the best areas to live in. In 1968, it was rare to see a single woman living alone in an apartment. It was not the norm in the current culture but was becoming a part of the counterculture that had begun a few years earlier. Norma was the type of woman that inspired the Mary Tyler Moore show which soon gained popularity.

She was so excited to finally be in such a large and beautiful city that had so much to offer. There was every kind of shop and service that you could think of. She could go to a spa and get her nails done, or she could select from the latest in make-up and fashions to wear. In Norma's hometown, there wasn't anything like this. If you were to don the latest craze in clothing like hot pants or miniskirts, you would be shunned. She felt a freedom in Montreal that she never thought possible.

Norma also gained a lot of friends in Montreal. There were so many other young women like herself that wanted more from life than just to be somebody's wife or mother. They all seemed to understand what Norma was looking for out of life. This would give her a large amount of confidence that she never felt before. She became brave and started dating regularly and found plenty of men to date. They all were in college and smart, good talkers. Most of all, they seemed to treat her with a kind of respect that she never got back home. She would find herself going out on dates quite regularly, sometimes three or more a week. Everything seemed to be going along so good, but fast. This freedom soon would catch up with Norma.

It all started on the night of July 23, 1967, after Norma got back home from shopping in town with her friends. She told her friends that she wanted to get home early and not stay out late, as she had an early morning planned for the next day. But this was not the truth. She had set up a date with a man that she met while out at a club a few nights earlier.

As soon as she got into her apartment, she put on a new outfit that she bought earlier that day, touched up her make-up and quickly tidied up her living room. It wasn't long before the door buzzer went off. Her apartment had an outside intercom system where the guest could ring her room and she would have to go to the front door to let them in. So it would be obvious that she knew the man she was about to let into the building and her apartment. The man she let in would be in question for some time. It wasn't until 1972 that we find out who came that night for a date with Norma.

On July 25, she never showed up to work, and her friends started to get worried by later in the afternoon. It was about 430 p.m. that same afternoon that the police received a phone call from an anonymous man saying that a young woman had fallen ill and needed immediate police assistance. The caller refused to identify himself but left them with a specific address. It was Norma Vaillancourt's address.

When the police showed up to the apartment, the door was slightly open, so they went into the room calling out her name. There was no answer, so they proceeded into her bedroom, where they found her laid out on the bed, dead.

Although there was no obvious cause of death visible to the police, there were traces of blood on the bed sheets that suggested some sort of foul play. The police then called in the homicide unit led by detective Commander Andre Bouchard, who was a very well respected detective. He had solved a lot of murder cases for the Montreal police. He came with a forensic photographer who took pictures of the crime scene before anything could be disturbed by the investigators.

When they moved in to examine the body, they found that the traces of blood on the sheets came from strange wounds that were on Norma's breasts. There was blood coming from the top of one of her breasts. It was as if someone had bitten all around both of her breasts. But the bite marks would not have been what caused her death. The police coroner determined the cause of death was strangulation and that Norma had intercourse just previously to being killed.

The police searched the apartment thoroughly but came up with no clues. The only fingerprints they could lift were those of Norma. The door locks were not tampered with, and there appeared to be no sign of a break in. This led them to think that whoever murdered Norma was let in willingly, as if Norma either knew the killer or wasn't frightened of him.

Later that day, the police notified Norma's family of her death. They also wanted to find out if Norma was seeing any men, and what friends she hung out with. They began to canvass her friends and neighbors to find out who had come and gone to her apartment.

The technology back in the 60s was not able to trace the origins of the phone call. It was the police detectives thinking that whoever did call was probably the murderer himself. The police decided to keep the bite marks on her breasts from the media. But no concrete leads came from their investigation, and soon time passed and the case became lost amongst the now overly busy police force in Montreal.

There was soon to be much more that would take the attention and resources of the Montreal police department away from Norma's murder.

4

BALL OF CONFUSION

> *"Never in the Field of Human Conflict was so much owed by so many to so few."* – Winston Churchill

Although Montreal was the center of attention in Canada, having the best in art, culture and cabarets, there was a dark side to the city as well. Of course, there were the typical crimes and overcrowding issues found in most large cities, but that wasn't the biggest concern in Montreal. There were so many political and cultural issues that were centered around Montreal, like no other city in North America, let alone Canada.

Several diverse political groups coalesced in the late 1960s. The Separatist Movement re-emerged as a political force in Quebec in the late 1950s. The most important part of this rejuvenation was in March 1963 when the Rassemblement pour l'Independence Nationale became an official political party.

In practice, "separatist" is a term used to describe individuals wanting the province of Quebec to separate from Canada to become its own country. Supporters of the Movement preferred to call themselves "independentists".

Justification for Quebec's sovereignty was the claim of their unique culture and the French speaking majority of 78% in the province.

They felt threatened by assimilation of Canada by Anglophone culture, and the best way to preserve their language, identity and culture would be the creation of their own independent political entity.

The party then ran for election in 1966 where it received 9% of the vote in Quebec. This soon led to violent radical fringe movements, such as the Front de Liberation du Quebec (FLQ), to stage protests and conduct several attacks between 1963 and 1970. There was a total of 160 violent incidents that killed 8 people and injured many more.

The police were often called to disarm bombs, as well as deal with 100 protests per year during this time. The officers started feeling under pressure and overworked and wanted more pay. They were not given the same amount of money as the Toronto Police Department, where the Toronto Police Department were not under constant threat of their life.

MURRAY HILL RIOT – MONTREAL NIGHT OF TERROR

On October 7, 1969, the police officers congregated at an east end area for a "day long study session" which ended up being called the night of terror. The police ended up going on strike for 16 hours, and the city of Montreal went into a state of shock. About 2,400 Firefighters joined the walkout to support the police. Police and firefighters refused to work, and at first the strike impact was limited to more bank robberies than normal.

Police were motivated to strike because of difficult working conditions caused by disarming FLQ-planted bombs and patrolling frequent protests. Montreal police also wanted higher pay, commensurate with the Toronto police earnings. Guy Marcil, president of the union, said that the city refused to take the police demands seriously before the strike. A police commission report on the strike, later released, blamed the strike on "a deep frustration of members of the brotherhood, resulting from the breakdown of management-union relations."

The RCMP and Quebec Police Departments were then brought in to perform policing duties during the strike. Montreal police then attempted to block their colleagues' enforcement efforts by hijacking provincial squad cars, jamming radio frequencies that were used by the RCMP and vehicles that ushered other officers to the so-called 'study session'.

But as night fell, a taxi driver union, the MLT (Le Mouvement de Liberation du Taxi) seized upon the police absence to violently protest a competitor's, The Murray Hill Limousines, exclusive right to do airport pickups. Per the Montreal Gazette, about 800 demonstrators, not all of them cab drivers, descended on the Murray Hill Garage. Gunfire erupted between the armed protesters and security guards. Four buses were set on fire, and one of them was driven through the garage main door.

It was during this melee that a Quebec provincial police officer, Corporal Robert Dumas, in plain clothes was shot and killed by an unknown shooter. Another 30 people were injured during the strike. It was also reported that the striking police were aware that the taxi drivers were heading to the Murray Hill Garage but did nothing to stop them. In fact, when a convoy of taxi drivers were heading to Murray Hill Garage, the Montreal police acted and stopped Quebec provincial police cars that had been following them.

The result was shattered shop windows, where the trail of broken glass showed evidence of looting of several shops in downtown Montreal. With nobody to protect shop owners, separatists joined in on the rampage. Shop owners that were armed were forced to fend off looters. Restaurants and hotels were also targeted.

It was 16 hours of terror before the national assembly of Quebec passed an emergency law to force the police back to work. During the 16-hour strike, a police officer was killed and 108 people were arrested.

Even after the strike was over and things in the city resumed to normal, the police were still not functioning properly. They still had not resolved their issues with pay, and the bomb threats in the city were still going on, as well as the separatist protests. They were back to work, but extremely unhappy with the conditions.

The city itself was on a slow repair as well. It took a

long time to repair all the psychical damage, but what took even longer to repair was the cultural differences that had come to a head during the night of terror. Even though it was officially over, there was still a lot of blame that was being thrown around, and nobody was feeling at ease.

5

MURDER OF SHIRLEY AUDETTE

"A Book may be Compared to your Neighbor; if it be good it cannot last too long; if bad, you cannot get rid of it too early" – Henry Brooke

In the summer of 1969, Shirley Audette was 20 years-old when she moved to 1831 Dorchester, Apartment 2, Montreal. She relocated there from the suburbs east of the city, as she had several mental health problems and had been treated at the Douglas hospital. She was only 5'2" and 135 pounds and was not able to keep any kind of a job for very long. She lived with Kenneth Ehlert who was 26 and had been her boyfriend for about one year.

It was just recently that Shirley had found out that she was pregnant. Although she was known to have what some called dangerous rough sex with men that she didn't know, she was sure that the child was her boyfriend Ken's.

On the night of October 2, 1969, her boyfriend went to

work as usual. He had been working the graveyard shift for some time now. That left Shirley quite nervous, and she would frequently call him at work several times a night. In fact, that very night she called him at 3:00 a.m., and it was in that conversation that she told him about a very friendly man she had met. When he called her back at about 5:00 a.m., she didn't answer the phone.

She was known to have sat out front of the building quite often as it seemed to make her feel more comfortable than being in her apartment alone, so maybe she was on the front staircase. This is probably where she would have met that very friendly young man, who just happened to be her neighbor, who was coming back home from work.

His name was Wayne Boden, and he had been living there almost two years now. He was very polite to her and was so shy that he wouldn't look her in the eyes as they talked. He started by asking what she was doing alone out on the front walkway after midnight. Shirley then told him about how nervous she always was to be alone at her apartment when her boyfriend was away at work.

Wayne told her how nice the people in the building were, and he had never seen anything bad go on there. This was a strange thing for him to say, as he had never met anybody that resided in the building for the two years he lived there. But this gave her a sense of ease, and he was such a soft-spoken, clean-cut man. After a pleasant conversation for about a half hour, he told her not to worry, and if she ever needed anything to just come knock on his door. He then went inside to his apartment. She sat outside for a little longer, then went in to call her boyfriend again.

Shirley would also call all her friends every night that Ken was working, with mostly nothing to say to them; it was primarily to fill the time. It seems strange that a woman that would have sexual encounters with several men would feel so insecure alone at her apartment. Most of her friends didn't mind her calls, except that they could come as late as 3:00 in the morning. This was a time before answering machines and call display, so they would almost always feel obligated to answer.

The next morning when Ken returned from work, he could not find Shirley. His first thought was that she had picked up some strange man and decided to go to his place for a sexual encounter. This was only stated by Ken, and later the police never found any proof of this. Ken started to worry when she did not return that day. He then called the police to report her missing.

Early the next morning, the police received a phone call from the apartment building maintenance man where Shirley Audette lived. He found Shirley Audette's body dumped out back of the apartment building in an alley. The maintenance man never touched or moved the body.

Back in the 1960s, reporters would also hear reports of murders as they had police radios in their cars.

One such reporter, Steve Couch from the *Montreal Gazette*, overheard the call about this crime scene in the west end of the city. "I had my police radio in the car, so I arrived at the scene the same time as the police. We had a lot of deaths then, there was a murder every 24 hours. It was a hotbed of crime activity; in fact, how perfect to be a police reporter in Montreal, where a week wouldn't go by without somebody being shot or police shoot outs. It was like every morning you wake up there was another murder on the front page."

Shirley Audette was found fully clad in red wine flares,

turtleneck and a brown leatherette vest. According to Ken, this was the same outfit that she was wearing when he left for work. She was found fully clothed except for her shoes which were found in a courtyard out behind the building. Police figured that she was probably chased or was attacked by surprise, maybe while working in the garden or taking out the garbage. It was a very dingy, narrow alleyway where there were metal fire escape ladders and not much room to walk freely. This led to a small courtyard where the garbage bins were located.

Shirley was lying on her back with her upper body on the bottom of a drawn metal fire escape set of stairs and her lower body on the ground. Shirley had her eyes wide open and a weird smiling expression locked on her face. There was also some blood coming out of her nose, a sign that she had been strangled. It was later determined that she had been raped and strangled. She also had bite marks on her breasts. There were no signs of a struggle or any skin or blood under her fingernails.

She was also found to be pregnant at the time of death. Kenneth Ehlert told police that Audette had been involved in dangerous sex with some guy, which may or may not have been true; no evidence was found of this. She had no bruises on her body, and there was nothing to show that somebody had been rough with her. The police had interviewed many of the men who dated Shirley, but none of them stood out as having a motive to kill her, and all had verifiable alibis for the time of the murder, and no arrests were made.

Police then canvassed and searched the vicinity for any new clues, but came up with nothing. Again, the media was kept from knowledge about the bite marks found on her breasts. After these first two murders, in police circles there was a lot of talk about a serial rapist/killer which they nicknamed "The Vampire Killer". The public didn't seem very concerned and continued about their normal routines. It would be the next murder that would cause sheer terror and panic in the city of Montreal.

6

MURDER OF MARIELLE ARCHAMBAULT

"I see a Bad Moon a-rising, I see trouble on the way." – John Fogerty

---

Marielle was 20 years old, 5'5", 105 pounds, with beautiful blue eyes. Originally from Joliette, a small manufacturing town about 30 miles from Montreal with a population under 10,000 people, Marielle now lived at 3688 Ontario Street, Apartment 2, Montreal. She worked as a clerk at the Charbonneau Jewelry Boutique in Place Ville Marieas. This was in the same community where the very first murder of this nature, Norma Vaillaincourt, had occurred.

Marielle was enjoying the single life of a big city. She was thrilled with the excitement in the city and found herself staying out all hours of the night at clubs in the west end of town. This was something she never experienced in the small town that she came from.

It was one of those late nights in the club that Marielle met Wayne Boden. Only Wayne had told her that his name was Bill. He was really the perfect man for Marielle - proper, had wonderful manners, he would hold the door for her, order her a drink. Wayne was also handsome, well-built and very shy. He worked as a salesman and lived close by. She was quickly smitten with Wayne.

The next day when Marielle came in to work, she couldn't stop talking about this wonderful man named Bill, how he was very caring and respected her enough not to try and take her home the first night. She told her friend he was the kind of guy that she could take home to her parents in a very conservative, quiet town.

The excitement in Marielle's eyes was cut short. Within a couple of days, one of her friends received a phone call from Marielle late at night. She had told her friend that she was worried, as she thinks she got herself involved in something that she might not be able to get out of. After several questions asking Marielle to explain herself, she just hung up the phone. When her friend tried calling her back, there was no answer. The next morning Marielle went to work as normal.

Wayne came to visit her at work that same day, but he would only stay outside on the sidewalk. Marielle went out and spoke to him for a few minutes, then returned to work. Her coworkers had noticed that she spoke English to the man, even though her native language was French. She told her coworkers that he was the nice man named Bill that she had told them all about. It was only a short while before her shift ended, and she quickly grabbed her jacket and left with the stranger, who was still waiting outside for her. She would never be seen alive again.

The next day she did not show up for work, so by lunchtime they tried calling her at home but got no answer. Growing more concerned for her, they contacted her landlady. Her landlady, Emilia Lamarre, told the manager of the jewelry store that she had not seen Marielle, but would gladly go up to her apartment and check on her. When Emilia knocked on her door, there was no answer, so she put her ear on the outside of the door. There wasn't any noise coming from the apartment at all. Emilia then unlocked the front door and opened it slowly, all the while yelling out to Marielle that she was coming in. As there was no response, she continued into the apartment. As she headed to the living room, she first saw the outline of a body lying on the couch. She called out again, thinking that perhaps Marielle was sleeping on the couch, maybe sick with the flu or something. Still there was no answer, but she couldn't see very well as the curtains were closed and no lights were on. So, she went over to the window and opened the curtains, she turned around and realized that Marielle was not alive. She immediately ran downstairs and called the police.

It was a short time before the police showed up, and along with them were the reporters. This time the police didn't let the reporters in the apartment. When the detective entered the room, the first thing he did was check and confirm that Marielle was dead.

Then the next to enter the apartment was the forensic photographer, who took pictures of the scene before they started their investigation. Marielle had her housecoat on, and under that she was wearing brown pants, green shirt that had three buttons missing, and her bra had been torn apart. She was laid out on the couch with a pillow placed under her feet. It almost seemed like she had been placed there ever so gently. The room was tidy and did not look like it had been ransacked, and nothing appeared to be stolen. There was no blood on her clothing but some on her cheek. There were bite marks on her right breast and on her neck. There were no drugs or alcohol in her system. Cause of death would later be ruled as asphyxiation.

Because there were no signs of a struggle and her house was neat and in order, it led the police to suspect that she had known her assailant and probably let him in to her apartment. They canvassed the area and talked with neighbors to see if anybody had seen anything out of the ordinary, or had seen Marielle with anybody that evening. They came up with no leads or anybody that looked suspicious.

During the search of the apartment, police found a crumpled-up picture of a man in her dresser. They took the picture around to Marielle's family, friends and neighbors, but nobody seemed to recognize the man in the photo.

It was then that the police took the picture of the man to Marielle's work, where both of her coworkers identified the man in the picture as the same man that was named Bill, that had come and met her and later left with her from work.

This was the biggest lead the police had to date, and they decided to release the photo throughout the province, hoping to get a lead on the man known as Bill. The community started to call the man in the photo "Strangler Bill." Of course, this created a panic in Montreal – there was a handsome, charismatic man named Bill who was making friends with women and then killing them.

It wasn't long before the police were overwhelmed

with calls from people that thought they had recognized the man in the photo. Police ended up spending hundreds of man hours interviewing all the leads they got, but were unable to learn anything useful.

It was only a few months after the photo had been released to the public that some people came forward to identify the man as a good friend of Marielle's that had died years before any of the attacks occurred. This was to be the bell that you could not un-ring. For months, the public was looking out for a man named Strangler Bill, and this would be a major problem, for how could they now direct people's attention away from that? This would not be a great time to have the name of Bill. Especially if you were single and were going out to the clubs and bars to meet women. Could you imagine meeting a girl, buying her drinks and telling her that your name was Bill? This was the first time the public had realized that there had been three murders of women by strangulation in Montreal. Panic was now part of everyday life there.

So, the police found themselves with no leads and a rapist and murderer on the loose in the streets in Montreal, with everybody looking in the wrong direction for the killer.

MURDER OF JEAN WAY

> *"If you can see the light at the end of the tunnel, you are looking the wrong way."* – Barry Commoner

Eight weeks later, a third victim would be found. Jean Way was 24 years-old, 4'11" and 110 pounds, and lived by herself at 1850 Lincoln #203, Montreal. This was an upper middle class neighborhood of the city and considered a very safe area. She had recently moved from a small rural area in Newfoundland and was working for a bank.

Jean had been dating a man by the name of Brian Caulfield, a 22-year-old broker, for about a month. She met Brian where he worked at Robert & Gelinas Geoffrion when she was running errands for her boss at the bank where she worked. Their eyes connected the moment she walked in, and within five minutes, he had asked her out on a date. She had gone on several dates since then, but couldn't have him up to her apartment until she had fixed it up some.

On January 16, 1970, Jean was out shopping for the day. She was on the lookout for some new furnishings for her apartment. While she was out, she couldn't help but notice that in every store she had gone into, there was this strange man that would hide behind things and just stare at her. He seemed to be following her from store to store, and she even tried going into some random places that she wasn't really interested in going into, but she just wanted to see if he would follow her, and he did. Now she was starting to get terrified.

Back in the farming community where she had come from in Newfoundland, she had never experienced anything like this, and she didn't have her family to go home to. So, she decided she would stop and ask somebody for help. There was a couple that she was about to pass, so she stopped, but when she tried to show them the man that had been following her, he had vanished. They told her not to worry, it's the city and there are a lot of homeless people around the downtown, and they will do that sort of thing, so Jean carried on with her day. It wasn't long before she saw him again.

This time she walked into a photo studio and told the clerk, who was the owner of the store, that there was a man following her. She was scared and didn't know what to do, as she was alone and had no family there. She didn't want this man to follow her home. The man offered to call the police for her, but she declined, saying that she didn't want to bother them or make a fool of herself, you know, a small-town girl comes to the big city and is scared every time she sees some strange guy looking at her.

He told her that she could go out of his back entrance that led into the alley and that he would keep an eye on the front of the store and the road around. She decided that that would be great, and he guided her back through the stock room of the store to the rear exit and unlocked the back door for her. She thanked him and went on her way into the alley. He then watched her walk away and saw nobody following her or in the alley at all, and waved. He then went to the front of the store and out the front door to look around for anything that seemed suspicious, saw nothing and went back to work.

He would think nothing else about this event until later when he heard about the murder.

The evening prior to her death, both Jean and Brian had been out at a night club until about 3:00 a.m. and then had gone back to Jean's apartment, where he stayed for about four hours before leaving. The next day, Saturday, January 17, Brian phoned Jean at about 5:30 p.m. to set up a date for 8:00 p.m. that night. When he showed up, it was about 8:15 p.m. and he received no answer. He then thought that she was probably just running late. He then went to a local bar called the "Cock N Bull" and had a couple of drinks. He returned to her apartment at about 9:30 p.m. and knocked at her door, and again got no answer. When he tried the door, it was open, so he let himself in.

He went into her bedroom and found her sleeping and tried to wake her. He realized that she was dead, but her body wasn't cold. The grey wool belt from her housecoat was wrapped around her throat twice, but he had not noticed that right away. Caulfield ran to the police station to tell them of the crime. When they returned, they saw

Jean lying on her bed, completely covered in a green bedspread, except for her feet.

Police immediately thought of Brian as the key suspect as he was not only her boyfriend and the person who found her body, but also she had now been covered up with the green bedspread since she had first been found. They took Brian in for questioning, but within a day no longer considered Brian a suspect, probably because he had a good alibi.

They discovered clothing fibers in her left hand, which indicated a struggle against her attacker. The apartment was also completely messed up and things were turned over; an obvious struggle had gone on here. This was clearly different from the previous murders.

Again, the police canvassed the area and talked with neighbors and friends to no avail. To make matters worse, they then found out the identity of the man was the man in the picture of the previous murder of Marielle Archambault, known as Strangler Bill. He was found to be a man that was a friend of hers but had died years before. This put investigators back at square one.

8

GO WEST YOUNG MAN

"No Problem is too big to run from." – Charles M. Schulz

Calgary, Alberta, sits on the edge of the beautiful Rocky Mountains and, in 1970, had a population of about 400,000. This is a much smaller city than Montreal and over 4,000 kilometers east and considered much safer. The city is known for the Calgary Stampede and is considered to have a much more western feel to it, where country family values were at the heart of life there. This was all about to change and in more than just one way.

The seventies were the beginning of the rise of gas prices, which in turn created a boom in the city, where its population exploded by over 40%. This drew attention by everybody from not only around the country, but also around the world. This would be the place to come if you wanted to make money and get ahead. It was also a great place to raise a family, where crime was at a minimum.

Of course, along with the oil and gas boom and all the big financial possibilities came the influx of east coast criminals which caught the police force off guard, not only by the large amount of people that they had not planned on moving to town, but also the types of crimes that came with them. The city was getting far too large, far too fast for them.

Mixed in amongst the new 200,000 people that were moving to Calgary was Wayne Boden. He had found it far too expensive to stay in Montreal. His apartment in Calgary was twice as large as the one he had in Montreal, and half the price. In Montreal, it was so congested that you couldn't really have a car or drive anywhere, with parking fees of $50 per year for your car.

Boden quickly found a nice place to live near downtown. There seemed to be so much more room in Calgary, and far fewer people. The streets seemed empty compared to the 24-hour hustle and bustle of Montreal. He could find himself walking downtown and only passing a handful of people. At night, he could look out on 17th Avenue, one of the main streets with shops and restaurants, and see almost nobody.

Boden had a vivid imagination and could get lost in his mind thinking about the many great things that he was about to do in his life, and the new quiet surroundings helped with his fantasy.

Another thing that he really loved to do was drive around the city of Calgary, and the freedom he felt with no mountains around him, it all seemed so wide open.

Wayne also felt much more comfortable in Calgary as

he could never speak French well, and it was really the mandatory language in the province of Quebec. In the 60s and 70s, it was the peak of the separatists, who demanded that all business was conducted in French. With that came a division of the city that would regulate daily that businesses would only conduct business in French; if they didn't, a fine would be placed on them. This was known as the language police.

It took Wayne about six months to adjust to the new lifestyle in Calgary. He hoped that, with the move, he would leave his urges behind in Montreal. But they started to come back to him slowly, just as they had for him in Montreal. It always started out in one of his fantasy dreams that he would have at night alone in his apartment. They were like the ones he had when he was young back in his room at home.

He would be on a stage somewhere, and lots of people had come to see him. One of the girls in the crowd would catch his eye. She was a pretty young lady; she was smart, like the teachers that he had admired back at school. He would end up having a very good conversation with her, she would tell him how much potential he had, and that made him feel good.

That fantasy dream would then bring back a real memory. One like the time that he had met Shirley Audette. She was a beautiful young woman who had lived in his apartment building in Montreal. When they first met, she was outside on the front steps by herself, very nervous about being in her apartment all alone. He was returning home from work that night and stopped to ask her if she was all right.

She was very sweet and told him that he had wonderful

eyes. She was a good talker as well, she read numerous amounts of books, and was very current on the events of the day. She liked the same music as him. She had wanted to see the Doors so badly she would have done anything for tickets. Wayne suggested to her that he might be able to get tickets for their next concert and maybe she would go with him.

She was so excited that she had to run in and call one of her friends to tell her about the concert. She got up from the stairs and ran into the building so fast that Wayne didn't know where she went or what happened. So, he stayed on the front stairs to think if he had said something wrong.

Soon she returned to the front stairs where he was still waiting. He wanted to know what happened and where she went. She said she just had to go call her best friend. He was confused on what she meant, tell her friend, about what, him? He could feel himself getting angry just then without really knowing why. She noticed that he was upset, so she put her hand on his shoulder trying to calm him.

After that Wayne went all dark again; he can't remember anything that went on. The next thing he knew, he found himself standing over Shirley's body in the alley behind their apartment building. She was seated on the ground with her back lying on a set of metal fire escape stairs. She was still fully clothed. How did this happen? he would ask himself.

He quickly checked himself over to make sure that he was all intact and had all his clothes on. He started to head back to the front entrance to go to his apartment. While he was walking through the dark back alley, he tripped and fell to the ground. As he was sitting there, he realized that he had tripped over Shirley's shoes. How did they get here? he wondered. Then he thought about if he should leave them there or go put them where the body was. Just then he heard a big crash behind him. Startled, he jumped up quickly and ran to his apartment. He waited quietly for about a half hour to see if he would hear anything else or if somebody was out back and had noticed the body. After that, he realized that it was nobody and decided to have a shower and go to bed.

Wayne remembered being in bed that night, trying to remember what had just happened with Shirley and how she had ended up dead. No matter how hard he tried, he just couldn't get anything back of that night. Then he started thinking, was this the first time that this kind of thing had happened? He had had several of these blackouts before, all the way back to when he was in school. But he couldn't remember ever waking up around a dead woman.

Then he thought about the next woman he had this same type of encounter with. Her name was Marielle Archambault. She was another beautiful, well-spoken lady that he had met at a local bar in Montreal. Their eyes met as soon as he walked into the club. He found himself drawn to her smile and asked her if he could buy her a drink.

He couldn't figure out why he did it, but he told her that his name was Bill. Was he going to do the same to her as he had done to Shirley? He couldn't, he wouldn't, he didn't know what he had done to her for sure.

Before they knew it, it was very late, and she was supposed to go to work early the next morning. She had just gotten a great job at an incredible jewelry store and didn't want to be late. He then offered to escort her home. Wayne offered to meet her there when she finished her shift the next day, and he would buy her dinner.

He remembers being so nervous the next day that he called in sick and stayed home. He pondered on whether he should go and meet her or not. He couldn't help thinking back to Shirley and how she ended up dead. It took most of the day, but he finally worked up enough courage to go and meet Marielle at her job.

Wayne was still too nervous to go in and see her, so he waited outside of the jewelry store. When Marielle noticed him, she came out and asked him to come in and meet her coworkers and wait inside, but he refused. So, she hurried back in to finish up her shift.

After she was done, he took her to a nice restaurant, located downtown. It was an Italian diner she had mentioned the night before in the bar that she loved their lasagna. Wayne then smiled as he thought back to how much they had laughed over dinner. He couldn't remember much of the details, just the laughing.

The next thing he thought of was when they got back to Marielle's apartment. He was being a real gentleman and walked her home. When she asked him to come in for a coffee, he declined, but after more prodding, he accepted. Was Wayne being a gentleman, or was he just worried about what might happen that night if he came into her apartment?

The next thing that he could remember was ripping her bra off as he pushed her onto the couch. He forced her head up with his one hand and started to bite on her nipple. She was a fighter and started to scratch on his arms, so he had to hit her in the head. Every time she would grab him, he would hit her. Finally getting tired of the struggle, he grabbed her nylons and wrapped them around her neck and started to pull tightly until she went still.

As she lay there all limp on the couch, he got on top of her and started to bite her nipples; on the left nipple, he started to bite so hard that he was tasting her blood. This aroused him more than he had ever been before. He then raped her, all the while drinking her blood. This was a rush he had never experienced before. He felt so high and strong now.

This, the memory of this running through his mind, aroused him again. Now Wayne was feeling shaky and had to sit down. Had he really done all of this? Was this all real? He couldn't possibly do anything like this. He admired smart women. This couldn't be real. Then the face of Jean Way appeared in his mind.

Jean was another beautiful young woman that caught his attention when he was walking down St. Catherine Boulevard in the downtown of Montreal one day when he was scouting some new businesses that he might possibly sell to.

He couldn't help but notice that she was very authoritative when she spoke to the different shop clerks. It was like she knew exactly what it was that she wanted and knew what to look for. He recognized that type of buyer from his years of selling. She had done her research and knew what to look for in a product.

Wayne was far too shy to approach her and speak to her, but he was taken by her, as it was not normal. He came across that kind of smart buyer in a man, never mind a female. He decided that he would watch her for a while, and he started to follow her from one shop to another. He wasn't looking at her sexually. She was pretty, but he was more interested in what she was saying to people than her looks.

It was after about six or seven places that they had gone to before he thought that she was noticing him. But he had to be close to her to hear what she was saying. After all, he didn't just want to look at her. But it was when she quickly went into a jewelry store that he decided that he would hide in another shop.

He just had a feeling that she spotted him following her and he didn't want any trouble.

It wasn't long before Boden knew that he was right, as when he came out of the shop next door and started walking back towards his own apartment, he saw Jean coming out from the alley behind the jewelry shop. This time he would follow her and stay at a bigger distance so that she wouldn't notice him.

Jean was now startled from her encounter and decided to head back home. She kept looking around and stopping to look and see if there was that strange man or anybody following her. After a while, she started to feel safe again and started to think about where she wanted to go for dinner that evening with her boyfriend. It wasn't long before she got to her apartment and let herself in.

Wayne stayed outside and waited for any lights to come on in any of the apartments in the building. It was a small four-apartment brick building. It was just a few minutes after Jean had gone through the front door that he saw some lights go on in one of the units.

After about an hour, Wayne went to the front of the building and waited on the stairway. Shortly after he sat down, another lady was leaving the building, and he quickly grabbed the front door before it closed. He then walked the stairway down to where he had figured Jean's front door was. He had to come up with something to say. He was running through different scenarios in his mind when suddenly Jean opened her front door. She had a laundry basket full of dirty clothes in her hands. She was startled when she saw him and dropped her laundry. Wayne panicked and pushed her into her apartment, and she fell onto her back. She then started to scream, and he quickly jumped on top of her and placed his hand over her mouth. When he jumped on her, it knocked the wind out of her as well, making it impossible for her to scream.

As had happened in the first two encounters with women in Montreal, it all went black soon. The next thing he remembered was standing over Jean's lifeless body which was sprawled out on the couch. Again, there was blood on her nipples and coming out of her nose, only this time Jean's left nipple had almost been bitten right off her breast. There were also several bite marks on her neck.

Suddenly there was a big crash outside of his Calgary apartment, and it snapped him out of this dream-like state that he had drifted into for the past hour. He quickly got up and looked outside, and it was a car accident.

He went back to his room and sat down on the couch and began to wonder if the same blackouts and strange murders were going to happen to him again in his new home. This would bring him to tears as he thought to himself, what is wrong with me? The last murder that he committed in Montreal of Jean Way, he had stalked her, went to her apartment, and then raped and killed her.

When we look back at his vicious crimes, one thing that he never thought of as wrong was the fact that he liked to bite them hard. He was totally engrossed in having what we now call a sadomasochistic relationship. It would seem he thought this part of his attacks on these women was okay. He never sought any type of forgiveness for being brutal. He only showed remorse for the actual murders.

THE MURDER OF ELIZABETH PORTEOUS

"History repeats itself, first as tragedy, second as farce." – Karl Marx

The boom in the city of Calgary had created a lot of jobs for people, and this drew people like Elizabeth Porteous, a 33-year-old school teacher. She moved to town in 1968 and lived alone in a high-rise located in the downtown core. Elizabeth was well respected by her fellow teachers at school she worked in, and she really enjoyed being around the children. She often dreamed of the day that she would have a family with lots of children.

Elizabeth was on the lookout for the right man to start a family with. She was looking for a man that was smart and able to discuss intelligent things, liked to read, and perhaps would be a teacher as well. If he had good looks and charm on top of that, it was a bonus.

In Calgary, it seemed everyone that she had been introduced to was more into being a rancher or cowboy. It wasn't that she had anything against that type of career, but it just seemed that they weren't very interesting to talk to, or they wanted a woman that would just be a wife. Sit pretty and clean house, have some children. She wanted more than to be somebody's wife; she was looking for a partner. In the 1960s, Elizabeth, though she was good looking and worked a great job, was not sought after by too many men, and therefore she seldom dated. In fact, she had not been on a proper date for three years, before she had moved to Calgary. Most of her spare time she spent with other teachers that she worked with, going on a ski trip to Banff, which was a resort town about one hour west of Calgary. It was on one of those ski trips in 1971 that she met a man that caught her eye enough to want to date him.

Sometime during their first day there, they had split up but planned on meeting at the bar later that afternoon. While waiting for her colleague at a local bar, Elizabeth was approached by a young man. He recognized a sticker on her car which identified her as being from Hamilton. Elizabeth was relaxed enough to sit and have a conversation with him. It wasn't long before they were laughing and reminiscing over people that they had both known, and what a great place to live in Hamilton was. They had hit it off so well, they decided to meet up back in Calgary and exchanged phone numbers.

On the way home to Calgary, she was so excited that she just couldn't stop talking about him. Her coworker was very happy for Elizabeth, to finally see her going out on a date with a man that she was excited about.

It was about two weeks later when she was back at work in Calgary that she told some of the other teachers that she was going on a first date with this man that she met in Banff. She needed help going out and buying a new outfit for the date as she felt that she was falling behind on the latest fashions. She and her friends spent three evenings after work trying to find just the right outfit. Finally, she was ready, and it was the night of her first date with the man that had kept her mind occupied for weeks.

The next morning, she didn't show up for work, so the school tried calling her but got no answer. Some of the other teachers told the principal about Elizabeth's big date on the previous night and that it must have gone well. As time went on, later that afternoon still nobody had heard from her. Some of the other teachers that were friends tried calling and still no answer. One of them used to live in the same building and knew the caretaker quite well and gave the principal the number.

Then the maintenance man, Bill Mosley, went up to Elizabeth's apartment. They received no answer when they knocked on her door several times. They tried the door and found it to be unlocked, so when they opened the door, they saw Elizabeth lying semi-nude on the floor in the center of the room. She was in front of the doorway almost blocking the door as they opened it. Neither of them tried touching or moving her body, so they backed away and called the police right away.

Within the hour, the police were at her apartment. The first detectives were Bill Crabbe, a forensic photographer, and Rick Talbot. It was customary for them to take complete photos of the crime scene, centered around the victim and her proximity to things in her apartment. Detective Rick Talbot waited patiently as the pictures were being taken. The first thing that Talbot noticed was that

Elizabeth was in what he called "the rape position". Elizabeth was lying in the middle of the room on her back just behind the door with her dress torn open. Her apartment showed considerable signs of struggle. She was raped and strangled, and her breasts were mutilated with bite marks. There were buttons that had been torn from the dress on the floor, obviously from an attack where someone had grabbed abruptly.

The cause of death was not known from the sight of her body, but like the bodies that were found in Montreal, there were bite marks on her neck and breasts. But in Elizabeth's case, her right breast had 77 bite marks on the top of her breast, and three on the bottom. But the teeth marks had been made with such force that the teeth had punctured from the bottom of the breast up past the areola and had come out of the top of the breast. This was a far more vicious attack than the ones previously done in Montreal. The body was taken to the morgue for the medical examiner to search for any more evidence that might shed light on the case.

When the police dusted for fingerprints, they noticed that in the kitchen, the fridge and stove had both been wiped down. Somebody had obviously taken the time to wipe everything down before leaving the apartment. But one thing that the police found curious was that seven of the eight buttons that had been ripped off her dress were left in various places through the apartment, and one of them was missing completely.

Back in the morgue, the examiner had lifted Elizabeth's body into an upright position to remove her clothing, and out came a cuff link. It had been embedded in her shoulder where it left an impression. This cuff link had been left behind during the struggle with Elizabeth Porteous. The examiner also concluded that the cause of death was strangulation. Though they had the cuff link, they still had no strategy for finding the owner. The first thing the detectives decided to do was to talk with her family, friends and coworkers to find out what she had been doing the previous 24 hours.

It was when the police were talking with Elizabeth's coworkers that they learned of her first date with an unknown man that she had met earlier in Banff. Although few could provide any details of the man, one teacher, Harry Robinson, and his wife, by chance, had driven up beside Elizabeth on a busy road and were stopped beside her at a stop light on the night that she had her date.

They could describe the man as a 24 or 25-year-old good looking man, sharp dresser with neat short hair. Robinson also noticed that the couple were very caught up in talking and laughing, so they decided not to interfere by honking while sitting in the car at the stop light, and didn't bother to try and say hi.

They were also able to describe the clothing that Elizabeth was wearing, and they sounded like the same clothes that she was wearing when found dead in her apartment, or at least the same colors.

Also, Robinson, could describe the car as a Mercedes that was a powder blue color and roughly what year it was, as well as having a strange bobble-headed toy of some sort of bull or horse on the rear window sill.

Police ran a scan for cars that matched the description and so happened to find one that was registered to a man living only one block away from Elizabeth's apartment, the same one that she was murdered in.

The police then decided to put a surveillance team on the possible suspect and waited outside of his apartment. It wasn't long before Boden drove up and parked out front on the street and went into his apartment building. It was then that one of the detectives approached the car and looked it over. After seeing the bobble-headed doll on the back window sill, he decided to call it in to the detective's office. On hearing of this discovery, Detective Ed Madsen told the police officers to bring the owner of the Mercedes in for questioning.

The police knocked on the door of the registered owner of the Mercedes, Wayne Boden, a 24-year-old mild-mannered salesman with no previous criminal record. Wayne answered the door and, although he was not told the nature of the investigation, agreed to come along with the police to the station for questioning.

When the detectives came into the interview room, the first question they asked Wayne was if he knew Elizabeth Porteous. Boden responded by telling them that he did, and they had been out together on a date, and he seemed very calm, not upset at all about the question. He also claimed that after the date finished, he had left her at her apartment alone. Detective Madsen decided to take a chance.

The detective then asked Boden if he had lost anything and, not expecting it, he responded, as a matter of fact, I lost my cuff link. Then Madsen showed Boden the cuff link that they had found earlier in her apartment. He said it was his, in fact, it was given to him by his mother, who had passed it down from her grandmother.

Shortly after, the detectives arrested Boden and placed him into custody. Even though he had been arrested, he claimed that he was innocent and just lost the cuff link at her place before she was murdered. The police feared that they would not be able to convict him with such limited evidence. They needed to strengthen their case with more evidence.

Detective Madsen just happened to be reading that the British police were involved in a case where bite marks had been identified and clearly established the identity of the person responsible for the crime. In Canada, such evidence had never been used in court before. Madsen went to their lead pathologist, Dr. Reynolds, who in turn recommended a qualified orthodontist, Dr. Gordon Swann. After finding Dr. Swann, they asked Wayne Boden if he would submit to a dental impression. He agreed without hesitation, still claiming his innocence. Madsen couldn't figure out exactly why Boden would so easily let them take the impressions, except for maybe he thought that it wouldn't be able to prove anything. After all, this was not the kind of thing the public had ever heard about, not even in the crime shows of the day such as Hawaii Five-0.

Gordon Swann then wrote to the FBI, which was led by Director J. Edgar Hoover back then, and said that they had never done any kind of procedure with dental impressions. Dr. Swann turned his attention to England, where Detective Madsen had read about them using such evidence. Swann was very pleased to learn that the British cops had already had convictions using dental impressions.

While waiting for the results of the detailed dental impression, the police then discovered that Boden was relatively new to Calgary and was previously in Montreal. When they contacted the Montreal police, they explained to them of their recent homicide and about the bite marks found on the body. That's when they first learned about the cases that were similar in Montreal the years before. They now felt that they were dealing with a serial killer.

If Wayne Boden's dental impressions matched the marks that were left on Elizabeth Porteous's body, they may finally bring this vampire killer to justice. Only if they did not match, then a killer of five women would remain unpunished.

TRIAL OF WAYNE BODEN

"It's a great, great experience to finally get the reception that you rightfully deserve." – Kendrick Lamar

It was in May of 1971 that police in Calgary, Alberta arrested Wayne Boden, a young man that they believed had been behind a string of sadistic murders in two separate cities, Montreal and Calgary. In at least three of the cases, bite marks were left on the body, and police were waiting for the dental impressions of Wayne Boden.

During this time, detectives continued to press Boden for a confession. They would press him for hours at a time, but Boden would keep a calm composure and continued to claim his innocence. This planted some doubt into the detectives' minds as to whether they had the right man. Boden never seemed to get upset or annoyed by the hours of interrogation, a peaceful character he maintained.

Outside of the interrogation, other detectives came up with a new clue. While searching Boden's apartment, they found the one missing button from Elizabeth Porteous's dress. At the same time, the preliminary results of the dental impression came back as a match.

Now confronted with the mounting evidence, Wayne Boden's defences began to crumble. I think that he may have thought that there would have been no way to match the dental impression to the bite marks left on the body.

Within a week, Wayne Boden finally confessed to the murder of Elizabeth Porteous. He told them something to the effect that when he drove her home, he snapped and couldn't remember what happened. He had also told the Calgary police that he had committed three of the murders in Montreal.

Finding out about this new information, Detective Ernie Reimer called the Montreal Police Service to tell them about the murder in Calgary and the man that they had in their custody.

Detective Reimer spoke with Commander Andre Bouchard, who was quite familiar with Montreal's own Vampire Rapist and immediately decided to send two of the detectives that had been assigned to the now cold case to Calgary. Within the week, the two Montreal detectives arrived in Calgary to begin their questioning of Boden about the killings that had happened years earlier in their city.

When he confessed, he denied any involvement in the murder of Norma Vaillaincourt, the very first victim in Montreal. Wayne also claimed that he never sexually assaulted any of his victims and that any sexual activity that he had with the women was consensual. It was suggested that he did not want to be put in prison as a known rapist as they don't fare as well as just murderers.

On February 14, 1972, Wayne Boden appeared in the Alberta Supreme Court for the murder of Elizabeth Porteous. Even though he had confessed to police, he withdrew his confession and pled not guilty. The prosecution made judicial history in Canada with this case by introducing the match between Wayne Boden's teeth and the bite marks on the bodies. This was also the prosecution's strongest piece of evidence in the case. The display went extremely well by showing how easily the teeth fell into place over the pictures of the bite marks, and Swann could demonstrate 29 points where Boden's teeth matched the marks on Elizabeth's body. The actual trial only lasted two-and-a-half days. It only took the jury two hours to reach a guilty verdict, and Wayne Boden was sentenced to life in prison.

The public were very relieved and happy over the results. Finally, "Strangler Bill" or "The Vampire Killer" had finally been caught and put away for life.

Later in 1972, Boden faced a Montreal court for the killings that had happened there. This time Wayne pled guilty to three of the murders and received three additional life sentences.

He was not convicted of the first murder of Norma Vaillaincourt in Montreal. Another person, Raymond Suave, was convicted for her murder in 1994 and sentenced to 10 years in prison.

THE MURDER OF ELIZABETH (IN BODEN'S MIND)

When Wayne remembers Elizabeth Porteous's murder, it reads like the first three women that he murdered in Calgary. Only in his mind, he thought that Elizabeth was the perfect woman for him. Not only was she smart and pretty, she was a teacher as well. That was the ultimate catch for him.

Wayne spotted a sticker on the back of Elizabeth's car when it was parked out on 17th Avenue, the same street where he lived. The sticker was that of the Hamilton Tiger Cats, a professional football team in Hamilton, where he grew up. He had not seen that on a car since he was a kid, and it gave him a gleam of excitement.

He waited by the car to see who was driving it; maybe he even knew the person. After only about 15 minutes, he saw Elizabeth come out to her car, get in and drive away. Getting caught up in a rush of excitement, he jumped into his Mercedes, which had been parked only two spots behind, and followed her.

Elizabeth drove to the school that she worked at and parked in the teachers' parking area. She exited the car and went into the main office of the school. He slowly got out of his car and walked over to where she had parked. He closely looked through her windows onto the front passenger seat, where a pile of papers had scattered across the seat and onto the floor.

He wanted to see if there was something with the woman's name on it or, even better, perhaps her address. Checking to make sure that nobody else had noticed what he was doing, he pressed his face against the passenger side window but still couldn't quite see anything.

He then tried the passenger door, but it was locked. He moved across to the driver's side door and tried it. This one was unlocked. So again, looking over his shoulder to make sure there was nobody around, he opened the door and got into the front seat. From the front seat, he could go through Elizabeth's papers to find out the information that he needed.

It wasn't long before he noticed that these were tests that were graded and marked by the woman; she must be a teacher at the school. He then opened the glove compartment in the car to see if there were any papers there that might help. Out came an insurance policy that had a name at the top of the contract; it said Elizabeth Porteous. It also gave an address and phone number. He quickly grabbed the papers and exited the car and went back to his own car. Now that he had a name and address, what was he going to do with them?

That night after Wayne got back home and retired to bed, he started to have his usual dreams that he always instigated on himself. He was a larger-than-life singer on a stage performing to a room full of women who were all very pretty and found him adorable. He would then catch the eye of one of the pretty girls, only this time it was the face of Elizabeth that was looking at him. It was the woman he had seen earlier. Could this be a sign? Was he supposed to contact her? Was she entering his dreams for a reason?

Wayne tossed and turned all night. He couldn't stop thinking about Elizabeth, and how she had come into his dreams and happened to be on 17th Street earlier, with her

Hamilton Tiger Cats sticker. Maybe she had put it there for him? But he had to find out if she was married, or if she lived with someone. The next day, he searched out her apartment in downtown Calgary. He was not happy to find out that she was living in a high-rise apartment. When he went to the front door, there was a doorman there. How would he be able to get in and get out without the doorman noticing him? He got back into his car drove away very puzzled. How was he going to do this? Instead of driving back to his home, he drove to the school where Elizabeth worked. He pulled into the front parkway and sat without the radio on or the car running. He just sat in silence focused on planning on how to get to Elizabeth.

It was about an hour later when he realized that in the teachers' parking lot, Elizabeth's car wasn't there. Where could she be? It was a school day, after all, and shouldn't a teacher be teaching? He then decided he would go into the school and walk around. He didn't know why he was going to do this; he just knew that he had to do something. He found himself going up and down the halls, just wandering aimlessly with no direction planned.

Suddenly a bell went off across the loud speaker, and with a quick swoosh the doors to all the different classrooms swung open and a parade of children came running out of the rooms. The quiet hallways suddenly became alive with all the screaming, laughing and running around from the children.

It was then that a group of kids ran right into Wayne so hard that two of them fell backwards onto the floor. They weren't hurt and, in fact, were laughing and apologized to Wayne rather quickly. He let them know it was okay and that he didn't mind at all. When one of the kids asked him if he was lost, Wayne's mind quickly thought, this could be the perfect opportunity, so he told them yes, and asked if they knew who Mrs. Porteous was and which class room she had taught in. They all laughed again, and one of them informed Wayne that it was only Miss Porteous, as she wasn't married, and told him what room she taught in, then went about to their lockers to get ready for the next class.

Wayne then found where Elizabeth's class was and waited outside as there was nobody in the room. Shortly after, an older woman came to the door of the class room and started to open it, and he excused himself and asked her where Miss Porteous was. The lady turned to him and told him that she was off that day and that she wouldn't be back until next week, that she had gone to Banff for a special trip with other teachers. He thanked her and quickly got back to his car.

Without even stopping back at his apartment, he headed out for Banff. It was a good hour or more to get there. He didn't even know what he was going to do when he got there, or how he would find Elizabeth. He just knew that he had to do it.

When he arrived in Banff, he parked at a motel and went into the office to check for a vacancy. It just so happened that they didn't have any because of a group of teachers that had booked the place up for a couple of days. He was thinking that he was meant to have found her, and that he did the right thing in driving to Banff. The clerk told him of another hotel not far away that was similar in price and he thought for sure they would have vacancies.

Wayne quickly left and headed to the hotel to get checked in and plan his next move. After he was in his room, he realized that the first hotel he had gone to, that had all the teachers booked into it, had a bar on the main floor. He then decided that he would go there and wait to see if Elizabeth would come into the bar.

He went to the bar, had his dinner there, and waited for hours. Just after midnight, he went out walking around the hotel parking lot to see if he could find Elizabeth's car. It wasn't long before he spotted it – it was easy to find having that Hamilton Tiger Cats sticker on the back bumper – then went back to his own hotel and went to bed where he would have another fantasy dream with Elizabeth being the main star.

The next day, he went back to the same bar and had his lunch. Only this time, who would show up but Elizabeth! She was seated alone and had a cocktail. Wayne got up and approached her by asking her if she was the one who had the Hamilton Tiger Cats sticker on her car. She was surprised but proudly told him it was hers, and she grew up there.

It wasn't long before they were sitting together and reminiscing about a lot of people from Hamilton that they both knew. They hit it off right away, and she told Wayne that one of her best friends was going to be meeting her at the bar shortly and she would love him to meet her. This made him nervous as he didn't want to be known by any of her friends in case Elizabeth ended up like the last three girls he tried to date. He told her that he was late for a meeting and had to leave, so they exchanged phone numbers and planned to meet up back in Calgary soon.

Over the next two weeks, Wayne was dealing with a guilty feeling that continued to follow him around all day and night. Even when he went to bed and tried to have his normal dream of being a famous star on the stage, he kept seeing Elizabeth in the audience watching him. After talking with her, he knew she was an incredible woman, and he didn't want to see her get hurt. Every morning, he woke up and avoided calling her by taking on lots of extra jobs at his work.

It was in about the middle of the month of May when his phone rang, and when he answered, it was Elizabeth on the other end saying hi and asking him how he had been. He paused, not knowing what he could say to keep her away from him. She went on to ask if everything was okay, and just for the few seconds that he had heard her voice, he knew that he couldn't resist. He reassured her that everything was great, and he was just preoccupied with work but very glad to hear from her.

By the end of the phone call, what he had hoped wouldn't happen, did. They had set up a dinner date for the following Friday. As he sat on his couch, he felt like he had been hit by a bus. He was stunned and he couldn't move. The thought of how he could stop this date from happening was running through his mind, over and over, how could he not make the date without hurting her.

Finally, the Friday came upon Wayne, and he had not yet figured out a way to get out of the date, so when he got home from work, he showered and dressed for dinner. At about 6:00 p.m. that evening, he headed over to Elizabeth's apartment and parked out front. What was he going to say, or do? He went to her front door and buzzed. Soon the doorman opened the main entrance for him and directed him towards a large comfortable sofa that was placed in the lobby. He told Wayne that Miss Porteous would be right down. It was very common for doormen in large high-rise apartments that were in good neighborhoods.

Within about ten minutes, she appeared out of the elevator and greeted Wayne with a small kiss on his cheek. It surprised him and he started to shake. She then smiled and told him how good it was to see him again and that she couldn't wait to talk about their old home town of Hamilton.

He took her to a very romantic bistro not far away from her apartment. They spent four hours talking, laughing and enjoying the six-course dinner that was served to them. But as the bistro was starting to close, she told Wayne that she was having such a great time that she didn't want it to end. Even though it was in May, Calgary, being in the prairies, was still very cold at night. She invited him back to her place for a night cap. He willingly accepted, then they both got into his car and left for her apartment.

It was probably then that Elizabeth's coworker, Harry Robinson, and his wife had driven up beside them at a stop light on the downtown strip. It was later their description of Wayne and his car that led the police to find, arrest, and later convict him for Elizabeth's murder.

It was later that night when they were back at her apartment, with the two of them sitting on her couch having a cocktail, that Wayne suddenly went all blank and started to attack Elizabeth. He quickly grabbed her by the blouse with enough force to not only rip about 10 or 11 buttons off, it also tore her bra right off her body. She let out a shriek and he put his hand over her mouth and pushed her head into the arm of the couch.

He started to choke her with her face still facing into the couch arm, and she soon started to gurgle and choke. He kept pressing with all his might until she finally stopped moving. He then let go of her and she went limp. He noticed blood on his hands and not knowing where it came from until he saw that his glass must have fallen and broken in the scuffle. So, he headed for her bathroom to wash his hands.

While in the bathroom, he thought that he had better wipe the fridge handle as he had opened it for Elizabeth when she was pouring the drinks earlier. He grabbed a clean towel, and just then he heard her moan.

Without giving a second thought to it, he then grabbed her housecoat belt from off the back of the bathroom door and went out to the living room again. He saw her moving around on the couch, still not sitting up, and he stood behind her and wrapped the belt around her neck, not once, but twice, and placed his knee up against her back and pulled as hard as he could until she went limp again.

He then flipped her body over so that she was lying on her back, still on the couch. He started to bite on her neck and slowly moved his mouth down over the top of her left breast. He started with little nibbles, but by the time he was over her nipple, he started to chew.

He soon became obsessed with the nipple and started biting like he was trying to eat it. Finally, he could start to feel the hot, warm wetness of her blood come across his lips and tongue. He could taste her blood as it started to fill his mouth; the taste affected him like a drug. This drug made him crazy, where all his senses were coming alive. His head was full of magic, so much so that it felt like he could see things that he could never see before. It was all so clear suddenly, he could see his victim clearly.

He then wished he could stop, turn off the clock and live in that moment forever. He would caress her strong legs, and pet her head, slowly playing with her hair by wrapping strands around his fingers. He could smell her blood and would then drink more. He felt like he was on top again, as he did in the past murders. It was a rush that he could never get enough of.

The next thing he would remember was getting into his car and heading for his apartment. It seemed like two seconds for him to get home, he was so preoccupied with his evening with Elizabeth. He got into his apartment and started to undress, and it was then that he noticed that the cuff link on his right sleeve was gone. Could he have lost it at her place during the struggle? He never gave it another thought, which would end up being a big mistake for, as we now know, the police would find that cuff link pressed into her dead body.

He then took one of the buttons that he had saved from Elizabeth's blouse out of his pocket and placed it in his bed. He would spend the rest of his nights of freedom dreaming of his evening with her while sleeping with that button. It would soon be used as a key piece of evidence in her murder.

AFTERWORD

SADOMASOCHISM

SADOMASOCHISM

Sadomasochism is the act of inflicting pain on another willing partner and has been well known about as far back as the 2nd century. In Jean-Jacques Rousseau's *Confessions* from 1782, Jean bravely spoke about the masochistic sexual pleasure that he derived from his childhood beatings.

Giovani Pico Della Mirandola described a man who needed flogging to get aroused. Even the Kama Sutra, which dates to the 2nd century, mentions consensual erotic slapping.

It was Sigmund Freud that studied the psychology of both sadism and masochism in 1905. Freud believed that these acts were rooted in the psyche from early childhood. A popular belief was that sadism might possibly begin with an infant biting and chewing on the nipples of his mother. Though the child does not consciously remember this act in adulthood, he may have a subconscious memory of enjoyment from this act.

EARLY THEORIES

The first theory written about this kind of behavior was written in 1639 by the German physician Johan Meiborn in his *Treatise on the use of Flogging in Medicine*. Per Meiborn, flogging a man's back warms the semen in his kidneys, which leads to sexual arousal when it flows into his testicles.

In 1886, a compendium of sexual case histories and sex crimes called *Psychopathia Sexualis* was written by Krafft-Ebing. In this book, Krafft separated sadism and masochism, understanding them as stemming from different sexual logics. It wasn't until Freud that the terms were put together, as Freud observed that sadism and masochism are found in the same person. He understood sadism as a distortion of the aggressive component of the male sexual instinct, and masochism as a form of sadism against the self.

EXPLANATIONS

Sadomasochism is hard to understand. Even harder to understand is how it could go as far as killing the partner that is involved in it. Most obvious, the sadist may derive pleasure from feelings of power, authority, control and from the suffering of the masochist. The sadist may also harbor an unconscious desire to punish the object of sexual attraction for having aroused his desire or aroused his jealousy.

I believe Wayne Boden fits into this last theory. First, he would meet women and have a good interaction with them. In most cases, he would see them more than once, and really enjoy his time with them. It wasn't until the second or third meeting that he would end up becoming aroused and attack his victim, almost punishing them for having aroused him. Once the arousal started, Wayne seemed to have no control over how far it would go. We see evidence of this in not only the savage bite marks on his victims' bodies, but by their struggles. He would start to have intimate acts with them and would get too aggressive; they would resist, which would only play into his desire to hurt them.

SADOMASOCHISM IN 2017

Recently there have been many cases of sadomasochism making their way into the news. In reviewing these cases from all over the world, the courts seem to be treating sadomasochism as a disease more than a crime.

One such case was in October of 2015. Another humble, handsome and shy man was convicted of the same type of crime that Wayne Boden had been found guilty of. Only with this case, it was a US Marine by the name of Sgt. Louis Ray Perez. The difference being Louis had two accomplices that helped him carry out the murder.

Louis picked up 22-year-old Brittany Killgore for a dinner date in the harbor in San Diego, California. Killgore never made it to her dinner with the Marine. Instead the sergeant and two accomplices kidnapped and tortured her in a sadomasochism sex ring. A dungeon was found where they believe Killgore was murdered. Also found in the dungeon were whips, restraints, zip ties, swords, a machete, black spiked gloves, a Taser, and a black knife that had been labeled "The Black Defender" by *NBC San Diego*.

We also see cases being reported that involve a woman who initiates the same behavior that Wayne Boden was involved in.

Another widely-reported case was the murderer Joanna Dennehy who was diagnosed with paraphilia sadomasochism. Dennehy, of Peterborough, England, admitted to murdering Lucas Slaboszewski, 31, John Chapman, 56, and Kevin Lee, 48. Their bodies were found in ditches in Cambridgeshire, England in 2013. She also pled guilty to the attempted murders of Robin Bereza and John Rogers, whom she randomly selected and stabbed in the street in Hereford. They were injured but survived.

Paraphilia is defined as a condition of abnormal sexual desires. The jury was told that some people prefer to be the recipient of pain or humiliation in sadomasochism acts, while others preferred to provide it.

Dennehy was put under psychiatric care rather than prison. She was given treatment for the diagnosis with therapy and medication.

Does this mean that we now look at situations involving sadomasochism as a medical condition and not a crime? Or does it mean that since we now have a medical diagnosis for it, we can label it and treat it differently than with only imprisonment?

EPILOGUE

"You cannot escape the Responsibility of Tomorrow by Evading Today." – Abraham Lincoln

---

It started out as a beautiful spring in Montreal in May of 1984. The weather was already reaching above average temperatures. All the street cafes were open and people were out in large numbers already. There was a really different atmosphere to the city than there was back in the 1960s. The fashion was made up of big hair and shoulder pads like the ones seen on popular shows of the time like *Dynasty* and *Falcon Crest*. No longer did the folk or groovy sounds of the 60s like the Beatles and Simon & Garfunkel fill the air, as the popular music was now groups like Duran Duran and Wham. There was no longer the innocence that was very much alive in the 60s.

On a beautiful day in May, Gloria Newsome and her best friend Rita Jones had the day off and needed a break.

They were both school teachers and had worked very hard getting prepared for the graduation time about to happen. It was a Saturday and they decided to go to a local market and shop around for some fresh food for their dinner later that evening.

During their lunch break, they decided to stop at a local bar and have a drink and a snack. It wasn't long before a man approached them and offered to buy them their drinks. At first Gloria was a little hesitant, but when the man pulled out his American Express card, she felt a sense of relief come across her almost instantly. You see, back in the early eighties, the American Express card was considered a card that only the very wealthy would have, so therefore, she thought he must be somebody important, perhaps a business owner.

After a couple of drinks and appetizers, the ladies had to continue with their day, so they excused themselves, and the gentleman, who had introduced himself as Bill, asked if they would be out later, and if they were, that he would be at this same bar if they were interested in joining him. Gloria thought the man was very nice, and handsome, a little rough around the edges, but that was kind of how she liked them. Gloria told him that she might come back out after dinner as it wasn't a school night and that she was a teacher. The man named Bill said that he loved female teachers as they were always so intelligent and had such wonderful conversations.

During Gloria and Rita's dinner at Rita's home, Gloria couldn't stop talking about this nice man that they had met during the day. Rita was a little more cautious and wasn't as smitten as Gloria was, but she told Gloria that she would come along with her to the bar later if Gloria wanted her to. Gloria had other things in mind and declined Rita's offer; she decided to go to the bar alone.

It was a local bar that was named "Cheers" on MacKay Street in Montreal that Gloria was going back to. It wasn't long before the handsome man named Bill joined her at her table. They spent hours talking and enjoying each other's company with plenty of laughs. Had Gloria finally met the man of her dreams? She didn't want to spoil it, so when Bill asked her if she wanted some company for the evening, she told him no, not tonight. Though he seemed disappointed, she quickly set up a new date for lunch the next day. He accepted, gave her a warm kiss on the cheek and offered to walk her home. She accepted and he took her to her front door, helped her unlock the door, and held it open for her. Gloria bid him a good night.

As soon as Gloria got into her apartment she couldn't even wait to take off her coat before she had to call her friend Rita. Though it was very late, Rita answered on the first ring and was excited to talk with Gloria about her incredible night out with Bill.

It was the next day about 11:00 a.m. that Gloria headed out to the bar. She thought that she could get a table of her choice before the lunch rush started. She selected a nice table far in the back of the bar where it was very private and a little bit dark. Again, it was only a few minutes before her new suitor showed up and found her at the back table in the bar.

It wasn't long before they found themselves all wrapped up in a great conversation and laughing, really enjoying themselves. Gloria knew that if he asked if he could come back to her place today, she would say yes. Time seemed to pass so quickly as the next time Gloria looked at her watch it was already 3:30 p.m. Where did the time go?

Suddenly there was a large crash and before she could even look up to see what had broken, the place was swarming with cops. What was happening? It looked like a small army was attacking the bar. People started screaming and running all over the bar.

She looked up at Bill and asked him what was happening. He had a real sad look in his eyes, almost like he was saying goodbye. It was only an instant that three cops jumped on Bill and wrestled him to the floor, then put handcuffs on him. Gloria screamed "what's going on?" several times with nobody answering her. They then dragged Bill outside and threw him into a squad car.

A detective then approached Gloria and told her that she had to come into police headquarters. A female officer placed cuffs on Gloria as well and took her out to another squad car. Driving in to the station, the car was extremely silent, and thoughts were running through her mind – what just happened, what did they do wrong?

After they reached the station, the female officer took Gloria into an interrogation room and removed the cuffs from her wrists. Still in shock, she didn't even hear the police woman leave the room. It was about a half hour before a male detective came into the room. He introduced himself and sat down across the table from Gloria. She was still so out of it that she couldn't register anything that he was saying to her.

Soon she realized the detective was telling her that she wasn't under arrest and that she had done nothing wrong, at least legally. But she was still confused. Then what just happened, why did they take her to the police station in handcuffs? The detective didn't know how to tell her that the man that had called himself Bill was an escaped prisoner. In fact, he was an escaped killer, whose real name was Wayne Boden, also known as "The Vampire Rapist" or "The Vampire Killer."

Seven years earlier, in 1977, Wayne Boden applied for and managed to get an American Express credit card sent to him in prison. How a life term prisoner could get a credit card is still not known. American Express has had an internal investigation to find out how this could have happened.

This was the same card that Boden had used to buy drinks for both Gloria and Rita at the bar on both days, as well as using it to pay for a hotel for the night he was away from prison. Boden must have had a way to to make payments on the items he charged over the seven years since the card was active and ready to use during his escape.

In 1982, Wayne Boden was given a day pass with supervision, as he was considered a model prisoner for the ten years he had been incarcerated, and it went well. The implication was that as a sex offender, he was given a particularly hard time in prison by other inmates and that it would be a humanitarian gesture to let model prisoners out.

In May of 1984, a prison director allowed him to go out with his art instructor and three guards as his earlier day pass in 1982 had gone well, and he still held his status as a model prisoner.

Both the police and public got a return visit from Wayne Boden. On that day in May of 1984, they had gone to a museum. Boden had been doing a lot of painting in prison. They went for lunch at the Mount Royal Hotel in downtown Montreal. During their lunch, Boden had asked to use the washroom, and the guards didn't want to stop eating and told him to just go. Boden escaped through a connected door in the Mount Royal Hotel washroom in downtown Montreal. Three prison guards were later disciplined for their negligence.

Boden later told the judge that he escaped because his grievances had been overlooked for 13 years.

Boden's escape led to a change in policy for outings for dangerous offenders.

In early 2006, Boden became ill and was taken to Kingston General Hospital. He was diagnosed with skin cancer and was confined to the hospital. Six weeks later on March 27, 2006, Wayne Boden died.

ACKNOWLEDGMENTS

Thank you to my editor, proof-readers, and cover artist for your support: Thanks, AL

Evening Sky Publishing Services (book cover), Bettye McKee (editor), Dr. Peter Vronsky (editor), Dr. RJ Parker, VP Publications, Marlene Fabregas, Darlene Horn, Robyn MacEachern, Linda H. Bergeron, Katherine McCarthy, Patricia Lenckus, Lee Husemann, Donna Destefanis

ABOUT THE AUTHOR

Alan R. Warren is the Host of the Popular True Crime History Radio show *House of Mystery* heard in Phoenix on 11:00 a.m. Independent Talk Radio and syndicated throughout the U.S. and Canada. It can also be heard online many different  places from iTunes, YouTube, Tune-in, Stitcher Radio, IHeart Media/Spreaker, Podbay, Podomatic and at www.alanrwarren.com

Al has his Doctorate in Religious Studies (DD), Master's Degree (MM) in Music from University of Washington in Seattle, Diploma in

Criminology from Douglas College in New Westminster, B.C., Canada, and Recording and Sound Engineering Diploma from the Juno Award Winning Bullfrog Studios in Vancouver, B.C., Canada.

He got his start on Digital Radio for the Z Talk Radio Network and still produces several shows for them.

ALSO BY ALAN R. WARREN

IN CHAINS: THE DANGEROUS WORLD OF HUMAN TRAFFICKING

Human trafficking is the trade of people for forced labor or sex. It also includes the illegal extraction of human organs and tissues. And it is an extremely ruthless and dangerous industry plaguing our world today.

Most believe human trafficking occurs in countries with no human rights legislation. This is a myth. All types of human trafficking are alive and well in most of the developed countries of the world like the United States, Canada, and the UK. It is estimated that $150 billion a year is generated in the forced labor industry alone. It is also believed that 21 million people are trapped in modern day slavery – exploited for sex, labor, or organs.

Most also believe since they live in a free country, there is built-in protection against such illegal practices. But for many, this is not the case. Traffickers tend to focus on the most vulnerable in our society, but trafficking can happen to anyone. You will see how easy it can happen in the stories included in "In Chains."

BEYOND SUSPICION: RUSSELL WILLIAMS: A CANADIAN SERIAL KILLER

Young girl's panties started to go missing; sexual assaults began to occur, and then female bodies were found! Soon this quiet town of Tweed, Ontario, was in panic. What's even more shocking was when an upstanding resident stood accused of the assaults. This was not just any man, but a pillar of the community; a decorated military pilot who had flown Canadian Forces VIP aircraft for dignitaries such as the Queen of England, Prince Philip, the Governor General and the Prime Minister of Canada.

This is the story of serial killer Russell Williams, the elite pilot of Canada's Air Force One, and the innocent victims he murdered. Unlike other serial killers, Williams seemed very unaffected about his crimes and leading two different lives.

Alan R. Warren describes the secret life including the abductions, rape and murders that were unleashed on an unsuspecting community. Included are letters written to the victims by Williams and descriptions of the assaults and rapes as seen on videos and photos taken by Williams during the attacks.

This updated version also contains the full brilliant police interrogation of Williams and his confession. Also, the twisted way in which Williams planned to pin his crimes on his unsuspecting neighbor.

REFERENCES

1. Burton, Neel: *Heaven and Hell: The Psychology of the Emotions*, 2014.
2. Burton, Neel: *The Philosophy of Lust*, Psychology Today, August 14, 2014.
3. Wellman, Kait: *Serial Killer Central*, July 17, 2010.
4. Crime Stories: *The Vampire Rapist 2006*, Aug 2, 2016.
5. *Quebec National Movement in the 1960s* – Quebec government website.
6. Sala, Paul: *Proletarian Unity*, no. 20, volume 4, no. 2, Feb/March 1980.
7. findagrave.com.
8. Gillian, Brett: Leo Affairs, June 2, 2015.
9. Guttormson. Kim: Edmonton Journal, March 31/2006.
10. Ricardo, Monaco and Burt, Bill: *The Dracula Syndrome*, New York Avon Books, 1993, isbn 0-380-77062-8.

11. Montreal Gazette: *Doesn't look like a serial killer*, p.33, April 13, 1972.
12. Wall Street Journal, May 9, 1984, pg. 1.
13. Crime Library Profile 137.
14. coolopolis, 06/2008.
15. murderpedia, /2009.
16. Wetsch, Elizabeth: *Serial Killer's News*, crimezzz.net, 2005.
17. Morris, Steven: *Murderer Joanna Dennehy Diagnosed with Paraphilia Sadomasochism,* The Guardian UK News, January 28, 2014.
18. Briquelet, Kate: *Marine Convicted of Sex Dungeon Murder*, The Daily Beast, 10/21/2015, p.138.

www.ingramcontent.com/pod-product-compliance
Lightning Source LLC
Chambersburg PA
CBHW070937080526
44589CB00013B/1538